SHARKS

By Micah & Nora May

Library For All Ltd.

AUSTRALIA

Library For All is an Australian non-profit organisation with a mission to make knowledge accessible to all via an innovative digital library solution. Visit us at www.libraryforall.org.au

Sharks

First published 2018

Published by Library For All Ltd
Email: info@libraryforall.org.au
URL: http://www.libraryforall.org.au

Sharks
Micah & Norah May
ISBN: 978-9980-89-920-0

Sharks are fish. They are found
in seas all over the world.

There are many kinds of sharks.

The smallest sharks are **dwarf lantern sharks.** You could hold one in your hand.

The fastest shark is the
shortfin mako shark.

Mako sharks are bigger than
dwarf lantern sharks.

Most sharks have many rows of teeth. This mako shark's teeth are very sharp.

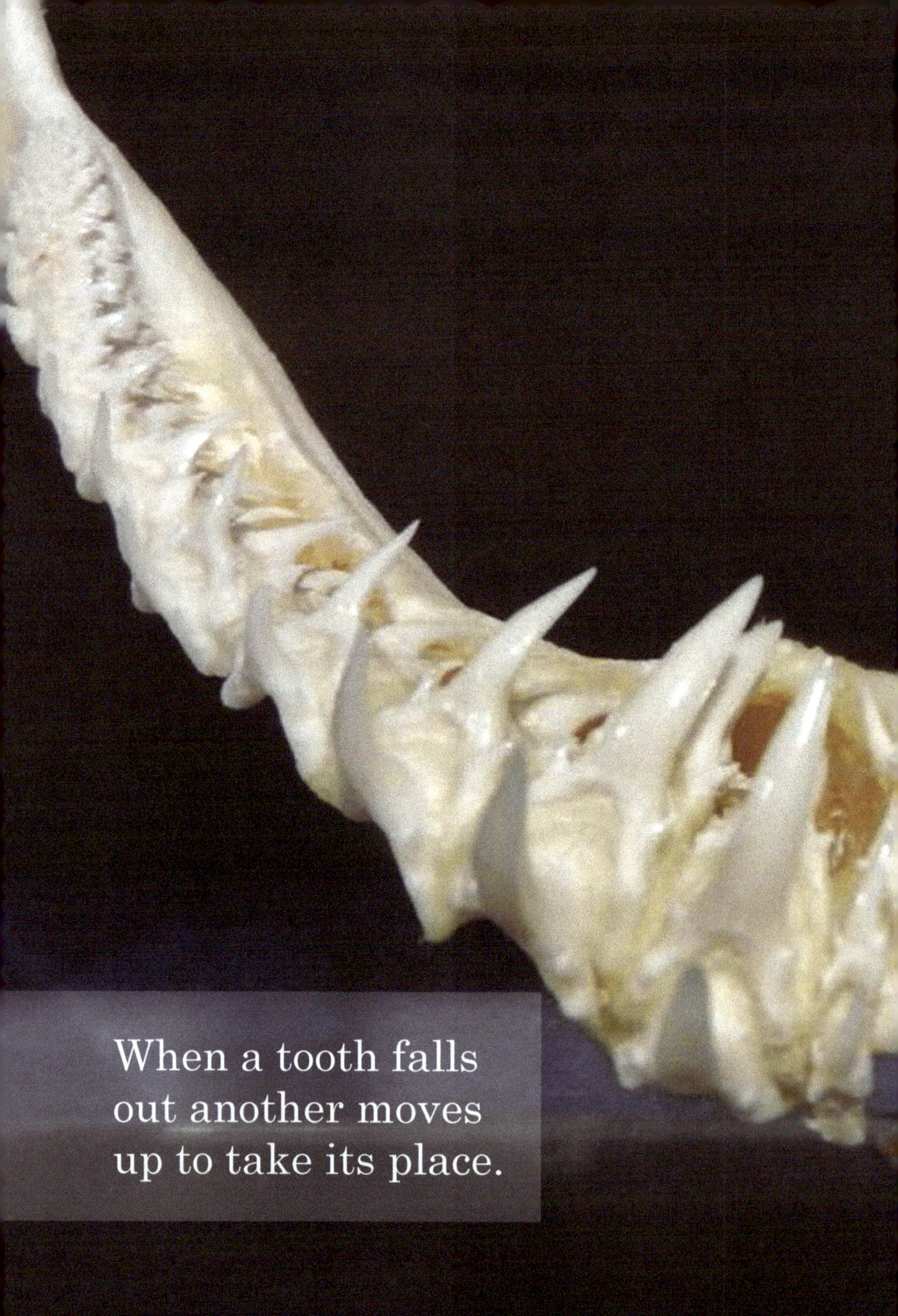
When a tooth falls
out another moves
up to take its place.

So sharks never
run out of teeth.

<u>Great white sharks</u>
are the most dangerous
sharks.

They have lots of sharp
teeth

Gills let sharks breathe under water. All fish have gills.

Most sharks have to keep swimming to breathe.

If they stop swimming
they will die.

Baby sharks are called pups.
When they are born they
know how to swim.

Mother sharks are bigger than
their pups.

The biggest sharks are **whale sharks.**

Whale sharks are not dangerous.
They eat tiny creatures in the
water called **plankton.**

Photo Credits

Domain	Courtesy of	Image	Copyright Holder	Copyright Information	Other Information
Wikimedia Commons	Hermanus Backpackers	Cover	https://commons.wikimedia.org/wiki/File:Great_white_shark_south_africa.jpg	The Wikimedia Foundation owns almost none of the content on Wikimedia sites — the content is owned, instead, by the individual creators of it. However, almost all content hosted on Wikimedia Commons may be freely reused subject to certain restrictions (in many cases). You do not need to obtain a specific statement of permission from the licensor(s) of the content unless you wish to use the work under different terms than the license states.	Content under open content licenses may be reused without any need to contact the licensor(s), but just keep in mind that: • some licenses require that the original creator be attributed; • some licenses require that the specific license be identified when reusing (including, in some cases, stating or linking to the terms of the license); • some licenses require that if you modify the work, your modifications must also be similarly freely licensed; and finally. • Content in the public domain may not have a strict legal requirement of attribution (depending on the jurisdiction of content reuse), but attribution is recommended to give correct provenance.
	Albert kok	Page 1	https://commons.wikimedia.org/wiki/File:Caribbean_reef_shark.jpg		
	Chip Clark/ Smithsonian Institution	Page 2	https://commons.wikimedia.org/wiki/File:Etmopterus_perryi_SI_cr.jpg		
	Mark Conlin, SWFSC Large Pelagics Program	Page 3	https://commons.wikimedia.org/wiki/File:Isurus_oxyrinchus_by_mark_conlin2.JPG		
	Spotty11222	Page 4	https://commons.wikimedia.org/wiki/File:Close_up_of_mako_shark_head_005.jpg		
	Pterantula (Terry Goss)	Page 5	https://commons.wikimedia.org/wiki/File:Great_White_Shark_(14730719119).jpg		
	Happy Little Nomad	Page 11	https://commons.wikimedia.org/wiki/File:Carcharhinus_obscurus_at_Seaworld.jpg		
	Zac Wolf and Stefan	Page 12	https://commons.wikimedia.org/wiki/File:Whale_shark_Georgia_aquarium.jpg		
	Derek Keats	Page 13	https://commons.wikimedia.org/wiki/File:Whale_shark,_Rhincodon_typus,_at_Daedalus_in_the_Egyptian_Red_Sea._(35827412321).jpg		
Flickr	Travis	Page 5	https://www.flickr.com/photos/baggis/6139383927	Our public licenses are intended for use by those authorized to give the public permission to use material in ways otherwise restricted by copyright and certain other rights. Our licenses are irrevocable. Licensors should read and understand the terms and conditions of the license they choose before applying it. Licensors should also secure all rights necessary before applying our licenses so that the public can reuse the material as expected. Licensors should clearly mark any material not subject to the license. This includes other CC-licensed material, or material used under an exception or limitation to copyright.	By using one of our public licenses, a licensor grants the public permission to use the licensed material under specified terms and conditions. If the licensor's permission is not necessary for any reason—for example, because of any applicable exception or limitation to copyright—then that use is not regulated by the license. Our licenses grant only permissions under copyright and certain other rights that a licensor has authority to grant. Use of the licensed material may still be restricted for other reasons, including because others have copyright or other rights in the material. A licensor may make special requests, such as asking that all changes be marked or described. Although not required by our licenses, you are encouraged to respect those requests where reasonable.
	Travelbag Ltd	Page 7	https://www.flickr.com/photos/98585738@N07/10346101216/		

Domain	Courtesy of	Image	Copyright Holder	Copyright Information	Other Information
PixaBay	StockSnap	Page 8	https://pixabay.com/en/ nature-water-animals- shark-blue-2570749/	Images and Videos on Pixabay are released under Creative Commons CC0. To the extent possible under law, uploaders of Pixabay have waived their copyright and related or neighboring rights to these Images and Videos. You are free to adapt and use them for commercial purposes without attributing the original author or source. Although not required, a link back to Pixabay is appreciated.	Images and Videos may not be used in a way that shows identifiable persons in a disgraceful light, or to imply endorsement of products and services by depicted persons, brands, and organisations - unless permission was granted. Certain Images or Videos may be subject to additional copyrights, property rights, trademarks etc. and may require the consent of a third party or the license of these rights.
	Wildfaces	Page 9	https://pixabay.com/ en/blacktip-hai- dangerous-1294753/		
MaxPixel	N/A	Page 10	http://maxpixel. freegreatpicture.com/Kobia- Whale-Shark-Underwater- Ocean-Fish-Divers-207401	The person who associated a work with this deed has dedicated the work to the public domain by waiving all of his or her rights to the work worldwide under copyright law, including all related and neighboring rights, to the extent allowed by law. You can copy, modify, distribute and perform the work, even for commercial purposes, all without asking permission.	In no way are the patent or trademark rights of any person affected by CC0, nor are the rights that other persons may have in the work or in how the work is used, such as publicity or privacy rights. Unless expressly stated otherwise, the person who associated a work with this deed makes no warranties about the work, and disclaims liability for all uses of the work, to the fullest extent permitted by applicable law. When using or citing the work, you should not imply endorsement by the author or the affirmer.

Glossary

Dwarf Lantern Shark
Smallest shark in the world.

Gills
Organs that help sharks and other fish breath under water.

Great White Shark
Deadliest shark in the world.

Pups
Baby sharks.

Plankton
Tiny plants and animals that float in the water.

Shortfin Mako Shark
Fastest shark in the world.

Whale Shark
Biggest shark in the world.

About the Author

Micah May is part time Director of Technology for Library For All Ltd and also works as an Ebook consultant for the Digital Public Library of America. He is passionate about helping libraries advance literacy globally. Micah received his BA from the University of Colorado Boulder and his JD from Harvard Law School.

Nora May is in third grade at St Columba School in Durango Colorado. She loves reading and her report in first grade about sharks inspired this book.

www.ingramcontent.com/pod-product-compliance
Lightning Source LLC
Chambersburg PA
CBHW040206160726
48006CB00014B/1918